JOB SEARCH & CAREER-BUILDING RESOURCE BOOK

2016 EDITION:

Free Internet Tools & Resources to Get a Job & Advance Your Career

1ST EDITION

BY JASON MCDONALD, PH.D.

© SUMMER, 2016, JM INTERNET GROUP

https://www.jm-seo.org/

0
INTRODUCTION

Everyone needs tools! You wouldn't think of being a carpenter without a hammer, a teacher without a blackboard, or a police officer without a gun. Accordingly, you shouldn't think about your job search and career-building efforts without an arsenal of effective tools to make your life easier. This **Resource Book** identifies the top free tools by category – ranging from tools to be a better blogger to tools to be a better Facebooker to tools to be a better YouTuber. All of the tools and resources are categorized, summarized, and ranked and direct links to their websites are provided.

This *Resource Book* is meant as a companion to my ***Job Search and Career-building Workbook***, available for sale on Amazon.com at http://jmlinks.com/jobs. The *Workbook* explains "how to" use the Internet to look for a job and build up your online personal brand image for career-building; the *Resource Book* is my collection of free, fun, and fantastic tools to make your life easier.

Free tools are fun to explore! During your job search, take a Saturday afternoon, and pull this Resource Book up in PDF format. Scroll through the tools, and check them out online. You'll find some you absolutely love, and some that you find silly or useless. But, best of all, they're all **free**! If you have a suggestion for a tool or resource, please email me via my website at https://www.jasonmcdonald.org/.

Let's get started!

CONTENTS:

» Resource Book Contents

» More Free Stuff and In-depth Training

» Acknowledgements

» Copyright and Disclaimer

►► RESOURCE BOOK CONTENTS

Tutorials – Online Job Search & Career-building Tutorials — pg. 5

Books– Recommended Books on Jobs & Careers — pg. 8

Personal Branding – Resources & Tools to Brand Thyself — pg. 15

Resume Sites – Job Search & Resume Upload Sites — pg. 20

Content Marketing – Tools to Create & Curate Content — pg. 24

SEO Basics – Tools, Tips & Tutorials to Master SEO — pg. 30

Blogs – A Better Blog & a Better Personal Website — pg. 38

LinkedIn – Tools to Schmooze on LinkedIn — pg. 42

Facebook – Friends, Family, Fun, & Facebook Marketing — pg. 46

Twitter – Handles, Hashtags, Retweets & Twitter — pg. 51

Other Networks – YouTube, Instagram, Pinterest, etc. — pg. 56

Monitoring – Content and Reputation Management Tools — pg. 70

►► REGISTER YOUR COPY OF THE JOB SEARCH & CAREER-BUILDING RESOURCE BOOK

Why register? Well, by registering you can access this document in **PDF** format on your desktop computer or tablet, making each link "clickable" to the resource identified. Many people buy this book in Kindle format, but it's a bit clunky to click from one of the free tools indicated in the book to the actual tool on the Web using your Kindle, so that's reason #1 to register. *It's easier to use it in PDF format.*

Reason #2 to register is that you'll get access to my **Dashboards**, which are the best tools laid out for you in easy-to-use format. These are the tools I use on a daily basis as I chart social media marketing success for my clients.

And reason #3? Behind door #3 are **free review copies** of my Workbooks (on SEO and Social Media Marketing) as well as email alerts when I release NEW and UPDATED copies of my fantastic, free, and fun Toolbooks.

To register, go to https://www.jm-seo.org/free and sign up for the email mailing list. Members of the email list have permanent access to the *SEO, Social Media Marketing,* and *Job Search & Career-building* Toolbooks for free!

►► MORE FREE STUFF AND IN-DEPTH TRAINING

Want more free stuff? *Gosh you're greedy.* But oh well. Here are links for help and more information:

- Jasonmcdonald.org (https://www.jasonmcdonald.org/) - my personal website, full of SEO, Social Media, and AdWords blog posts, information, and how to contact me with questions, comments, or concerns. Don't hesitate to contact me!
- The JM Internet Group (https://www.jm-seo.org/) - my corporate training site. Don't miss the blog, the free video tutorials, and other free goodies. All have lots of good insights into SEO, AdWords, and Social Media, including many free webinars and resource links.
- My Q&A blog at http://jm-seotips.org, where I answer incoming questions. Don't be shy: ask one.
- More free stuff at https://www.jm-seo.org/free. Be sure to take the free Webinars and register for my email newsletter on *Serious Humor*!

If you are interested in consulting services, in-depth social media marketing training, or just need a friend to talk to, call 800-298-4065 or visit the **JM Internet Group** website above. Consulting, classes, and books are reasonably priced, and designed to help you go from SEO or Social Media Marketing zero to hero.

» ACKNOWLEDGEMENTS

A labor of love, this *Toolbook* is also a labor of research, work, curation, editing, and the never-ending search for typos and dead links. Many thanks to Gloria McNabb and Noelle Decambra of the JM Internet Group (*my beloved wife, without whom nothing would ever really get done nor be fun*). My daughter, Ava, inspired me as a budding YouTube star, as well. My daughter, Hannah, who is nearly a Senior in college, inspired me to work long hours to try to pay her college tuition bills. And, of course, many thanks to "Buddy," my fearless Labrador retriever who accompanies me on the highways and byways of the San Francisco Bay Area. Buddy has an unlimited dog toy budget – yet another motivator for my quest to become a successful author. Thanks, everyone!

» COPYRIGHT AND DISCLAIMER

The task of Job Search and Career-building is an art, and not a science. Make any changes to your job search, career-building, or personal branding sites, posts, and general strategy **<u>AT YOUR OWN RISK</u>**. Yes, that is in **ALL CAPS** because it is **IMPORTANT**. The requirements, rules, and best practices change without notice, as does the behavior of Internet sites such as Google, Bing, Facebook, Twitter, Yelp, LinkedIn, Instagram, Pinterest, and all others referenced herein. This is a completely unauthorized work, with no connection of any type to be construed between it and any organization, publisher, website, search engine, job site, or social media platform. All trademarks are the property of their respective owners, and all content is subject to change without notice. Neither Jason McDonald nor the JM Internet Group nor the parent corporation, Excerpti Communications, Inc., assume any responsibility for the effect of any changes you may, or may not, make to your job search and career-building efforts based on the (perceived) recommendations of this *Resource Book*. Any changes that you or your organization make should be made at your own risk. By downloading and using the *Resource Book* you are agreeing to the terms of service: you are completely responsible for all changes you may, or may not, make to your Internet marketing strategy.

You are on your own, baby!

1
TUTORIALS

After a desire to succeed, a desire to learn is the most important foundational effort to a successful job search or effort to advance your career. How do you define yourself as a job candidate? What are the best careers out there? How do you build a resume, or ace a job interview? There are a lot of questions, and fortunately there are some really good tutorials and guides online to career advancement.

Here are the best free tutorials for job search and career-building!

RILEY GUIDE - http://www.rileyguide.com/

Founded in 1994 by a university librarian, Margaret F. Dikel (formerly Margaret Riley), The Riley Guide is the Web's premier gateway to job, career, and education information sources available online.

Rating: 5 Stars | **Category:** tutorial

JOB-HUNT.ORG - http://www.job-hunt.org/

The purpose of the Job-Hunt.Org website is to provide the best and most up-to-date advice from genuine job search and career experts to help job seekers be successful in the job search.

Rating: 5 Stars | **Category:** tutorial

JOB SEARCH AT ABOUT.COM - http://jobsearch.about.com/

About.com is a mega site about stuff (once owned by the New York Times). This subsite is a very successful component of About.com, focused on everything about job search and career-building. One of the very best mega sites and tutorials about jobs and careers on the Internet. (Can be overwhelming).

Rating: 5 Stars | **Category:** tutorial

QUINTESSENTIAL CAREERS - https://www.quintcareers.com/

This is a blog, a tool, a career site, a book, a mega site with information on job hunting AND careers. While many sites seem to focus only on job hunting and/or resumes, this site is neice in that it focuses as well on career-building. Check out the top tabs for job-seeker and career-changer, in particular.

Rating: 4 Stars | **Category:** tutorial

JOB HUNTERS BIBLE BY DICK BOLLES - http://www.jobhuntersbible.com/

Author of the fabled 'What Color is Your Parachute?,' Dick Bolles has built this mega companion site to the book.

Rating: 4 Stars | **Category:** resource

JOB HUNTING FROM NEW ZEALAND - http://www.careers.govt.nz/job-hunting/

OK, you're probably in the USA or Canada, but don't be so provincial. From many thousands of miles away, from the land where they filmed Lord of the Rings, comes an amazing job search guide. You don't have to be in New Zealand to use it, because of this thing called the Internet.

Rating: 4 Stars | **Category:** tutorial

GCF CAREER AND JOB CENTER - http://www.gcflearnfree.org/career

Use this nifty online tutorial on career planning, job search, cover letters, resumes, and many of the technical elements you may need if you are looking for a job or seeking to advance your career. A bit basic, but useful.

Rating: 3 Stars | **Category:** resource

THE ART OF NEGOTIATING - https://sph.umich.edu/careers/tutorials/negotiating/

Great Tutorial on how to Negotiate for that job you want. Not so much an over-arching tutorial to job hunting and career-building, but a very good tutorial on how to negotiate a better 'deal' in your job / career.

Rating: 2 Stars | **Category:** tutorial

VOCATION VILLAGE - http://www.vocationvillage.com/career-and-job-search-engines/

VocationVillage.com specializes in career coaching, counseling, and consulting. We are a location independent company founded by Janet Scarborough Civitelli in 2008.

Rating: Stars | **Category:**

CAREERONESTOP - http://www.careeronestop.org/resumeguide/introduction.aspx

CareerOneStop data directly on your own website. CareerOneStop offers a wide range of career, employment and education data as Web Services, allowing third parties to obtain quality-controlled data sets and seamlessly integrate them into their own websites.

Rating: Stars | **Category:**

2

BOOKS

While many authors want to keep you in the dark about other books, my philosophy is the more the merrier. There are many wonderful books out there on job search and career-building topics and, fortunately, no two are alike. Some are very "touchy-feely" and others are "micro practical." Peruse my list of recommended job search and career-building books here. Got a book? Email me with a suggestion, as the list is ever-evolving.

Here are the best books on job search and career-building!

CAREERS - http://www.amazon.com/Careers-DK/dp/1465429735/

Like visuals? This book presents a super summary of hundreds of possible careers in an exciting, lively visual way. Use it to help figure out what type of job / career you want. Excellent for that first step. In its own words, 'Covering more than 400 jobs, Careers is organized in an easy-to-navigate, clear structure that helps guide teen and tween readers. Check at-a-glance summary panels for chosen careers to learn about salary, working hours, training, and career paths. Cross-referenced job matrix tables offer another way to learn about all the options. Tweens and teens with no idea of what kind of job to look for can start with their favorite school subjects or hobbies and find relevant careers from there. It may not be time for your teen or tween to prepare a resume and find a job, but the advice in Careers can help young people start thinking about the future!"

Rating: 5 Stars | **Category:** book

STRENGTHSFINDER 2.0 - http://www.amazon.com/StrengthsFinder-2-0-Tom-Rath/dp/159562015X/

This mega best seller purports to help you identify your strengths, and be stronger. If you are seeking to advance in your career, it's a good idea to know your strengths and weaknesses, no? In its own words, 'In its latest national bestseller, StrengthsFinder 2.0, Gallup unveils the new and improved version of its popular assessment, language of 34 themes, and much more (see below for details). While you can read this book in one sitting, you'll use it as a reference for decades. Loaded with hundreds of strategies for applying your strengths, this new book and accompanying website will change the way you look at yourself--and the world around you--forever.' (Tom Rath, author).

Rating: 5 Stars | **Category:** book

WHAT COLOR IS YOUR PARACHUTE? 2016: A PRACTICAL MANUAL FOR JOB-HUNTERS AND CAREER-CHANGERS - http://www.amazon.com/What-Color-Your-Parachute-2016/dp/160774662X/

Richard N. Bolles brings us the 'classic' job seeking guide. 'What Color is Your Parachute,' is a traditional favorite among persons seeking jobs, or trying to find 'meaning' in their workaday lives. It's a bit 'groovy,' and in its own words, 'This helpful manual shares proven tips for writing impressive resumes and cover letters, as well as guidance for effective networking, confident interviewing, and the best salary negotiating possible. But it goes beyond that by helping you to zero in on your ideal job—and life—with its classic Flower Exercise. Whether you're searching for your first job, were recently laid off, or are dreaming of a career change, What Color Is Your Parachute? will guide you toward fulfilling and prosperous work.'

Rating: 5 Stars | **Category:** book

SO GOOD THEY CAN'T IGNORE YOU: WHY SKILLS TRUMP PASSION IN THE QUEST FOR WORK YOU LOVE - http://www.amazon.com/Good-They-Cant-Ignore-You/dp/1455509124/

If 'What Color is Your Parachute,' and other books often emphasize 'following your passion,' then this book is quite the opposite. Read both approaches, and figure it out for yourself - there probably is no 'right' answer. In it's own words, 'In this eye-opening account, Cal Newport debunks the long-held belief that "follow your passion" is good advice. Not only is the cliché flawed-preexisting passions are rare and have little to do with how most people end up loving their work-but it can also be dangerous, leading to anxiety and chronic job hopping.'

Rating: 5 Stars | **Category:** book

KNOCK 'EM DEAD 2016: THE ULTIMATE JOB SEARCH GUIDE -
http://www.amazon.com/Knock-Em-Dead-2016-Ultimate/dp/1440588813/

New York Times bestseller Martin Yate has helped millions of job seekers improve their job search and career management tactics, changing their lives forever. Featuring his unique, time-tested methods for achieving professional success, this brand-new edition provides you with the tools you need to win your next job and successfully navigate the twists and turns of your entire career.

Rating: 4 Stars | **Category:** book

WAIT, HOW DO I WRITE THIS EMAIL?: GAME-CHANGING TEMPLATES FOR NETWORKING AND THE JOB SEARCH - http://www.amazon.com/Wait-Write-This-Email-Game-Changing/dp/0996349901

This is a book about more than just email: about templates for all sorts of job- and career-related contacts and communciations. In its own words, 'In his comprehensive guide, career expert Danny Rubin provides more than 100 critical email and document templates for networking and the job search. With each template, Danny saves you time and takes the stress out of professional email writing. Page after page, Danny offers detailed instructions for networking (ex: how to contact alumni from your school) and the job search (ex: how to apply even if the company has no openings at the time). He also includes smart LinkedIn templates, memorable handwritten notes, the outline for a powerful one-page resume and a fresh cover letter strategy with a focus on storytelling.'

Rating: 4 Stars | **Category:** book

THE 2-HOUR JOB SEARCH: USING TECHNOLOGY TO GET THE RIGHT JOB FASTER -
http://www.amazon.com/The-2-Hour-Job-Search-Technology/dp/1607741709/

It's a bit old (published 2012), but it does emphasize the 'technical' side of getting a job, and securing that all-important first interview. In its own words, 'A job-search manual that gives career seekers a systematic, tech-savvy formula to efficiently and effectively target potential employers and secure the essential first interview.'

Rating: 4 Stars | **Category:** book

SHUT UP AND GO!: A MILLENNIAL'S GUIDE TO FIGURING OUT WHAT YOU WANT AND HOW TO GET IT - http://www.amazon.com/Shut-Up-And-Go-Millennials-ebook/dp/B01D6G0V6C/

This book attempts to wed the millenial's love of technology and action with the introspection of the 1970s 'do what you love' type of job book. In its own words, 'Combining a decade of studying, knowledge, and learning about inner discovery and accomplishing your goals, Shut Up and Go! is filled with practical tools, insights, and action steps you can take to craft an amazing life. While most books focus on where you should get, but leave you lacking a clear next step, this book provides the how to make it a reality. People all around you are living lives of fulfillment and purpose. You should be too. '

Rating: 4 Stars | **Category:** book

DO WHAT YOU ARE: DISCOVER THE PERFECT CAREER FOR YOU THROUGH THE SECRETS OF PERSONALITY TYPE - http://www.amazon.com/Do-What-You-Are-Personality/dp/031623673X/

If you've ever wondered what 'personality type,' you are, then this is a great job / career book for you. It's approach is based on the idea that you have a 'personality type,' and once you discover that, you can identify the best job / career that 'fits' that type. In its own words, 'The bestselling guide to finding career success and satisfaction through Personality Type is now thoroughly revised, expanded, and updated.DO WHAT YOU ARE--the time-honored classic that has already helped more than a million people find truly satisfying work--is now updated to include jobs in today's hottest markets, including health services, education, and communications technology.'

Rating: 4 Stars | **Category:** book

THE ART OF WORK: A PROVEN PATH TO DISCOVERING WHAT YOU WERE MEANT TO DO - http://www.amazon.com/Art-Work-Proven-Discovering-Meant-ebook/dp/B00PWOHB1U/

A touchy feely book about learning what you truly want to do in terms of your job / career, and then actually doing it. Excellent for that very first, passionate phase of job searching. In its own words, 'Jeff Goins, a brilliant new voice counting Seth Godin and Jon Acuff among his fans, explains how to abandon the status quo and live a life that matters with true passion and purpose. The path to your life's work is difficult and risky, even scary, which is why few finish the journey. This is a book about discovering your life's work, that treasure of immeasurable worth we all long for. It's about the task you were born to do.'

Rating: 4 Stars | **Category:** book

How To Find A Job: When There Are No Jobs (Book #2) A Necessary Job Search and Career Planning Guide for Today's Job Market (Career Development) - http://www.amazon.com/gp/product/B0056PFONW/

In its own words, 'Paul Rega introduces a revolutionary new concept in career management and personal development called Intuitive Personal Assessment (IPA). Paul takes his readers on a powerful journey as he tells a gripping story about his own career and the unique challenges he's faced as an executive recruiter. The author shares his vast knowledge of career planning and the inner workings of the job search process, citing hundreds of proven and effective job search techniques. He explains how to market your background to a targeted audience, interviewing skills and techniques, network building strategies, how to utilize personal and business contacts, effective use of social media, including LinkedIn, Facebook and Twitter, insider tips on working with recruiters, salary and benefits negotiation, how to write a resume, cover and follow-up letters, how to start and succeed in your own business and much more.'

Rating: 4 Stars | **Category:** book

Born for This: How to Find the Work You Were Meant to Do - http://www.amazon.com/Born-This-Find-Work-Meant/dp/1101903988/

Author Chris Guillebeau bring us this fabulous book on working better, smarter, harder and in a more fllexible way. In his own words, 'Have you ever met someone with the perfect job? To the outside observer, it seems like they've won the career lottery -- that by some stroke of luck or circumstance they've found the one thing they love so much that it doesn't even feel like work—and they're getting paid well to do it. To the outside observer, it seems like they've won the career lottery—that by some stroke of luck or circumstance, they've found the one thing they love so much that it doesn't even feel like work, and they're getting paid well to do it.'

Rating: 3 Stars | **Category:** book

JOB INTERVIEW TIPS FOR WINNERS: 12 KEY WAYS TO LAND THE JOB - http://www.amazon.com/Job-Interview-Tips-For-Winners-ebook/dp/B018VB6R24/

First, figure out what type of job you want. Second, search and schmooze for it. Third, get the interview. That interview is very important: don't blow it. This book will help you 'ace' your job interview. In its own words, 'On the hunt for a new job? This book will show you exactly how to ace your next interview. Learn what to say, how to act, what to wear, and how to prepare for common interview questions. Discover the questions you should ask your would-be employers, and how to present your strengths and weaknesses in the best possible light. Furthermore, learn eight ways you can immediately improve your body language - and understand how to make sure it doesn't sabotage you during your next interview. '

Rating: 3 Stars | **Category:** book

THE 4-HOUR WORKWEEK - http://www.amazon.com/The-4-Hour-Workweek-Escape-Anywhere/dp/0307465357

Timothy Ferriss brings us this amazingly interesting, fun, provocative and somewhat unbelievable book on working smarter. 'Whether your dream is escaping the rat race, experiencing high-end world travel, earning a monthly five-figure income with zero management, or just living more and working less, The 4-Hour Workweek is the blueprint. his step-by-step guide to luxury lifestyle design teaches"

Rating: 3 Stars | **Category:** book

THE CAREER CODE: MUST-KNOW RULES FOR A STRATEGIC, STYLISH, AND SELF-MADE CAREER - http://www.amazon.com/The-Career-Code-Must-Know-Strategic/dp/1419718029/

Career success isn't only for girls or women, so men, listen up. This is a book about entrepreneurship and careers by women for women, but full of interesting advice. In its own words, 'In this approachable, authoritative, and inspirational book, you will find the most useful and accessible tips and tricks to strategically build your career into exactly what you want it to be, from negotiating your salary to avoiding the biggest mistake most people make when they quit. Chapters include advice on résumé building, dressing for the job you want, and how to effectively communicate at work—even with the most difficult colleagues—all done with the Who What Wear girls' practical and polished signature style.'

Rating: 3 Stars | **Category:** book

FIND YOUR PASSION: 25 QUESTIONS YOU MUST ASK YOURSELF -

http://www.amazon.com/Find-Your-Passion-Questions-Yourself-ebook/dp/B00DIHO7NS/

This job book focuses on inventorying your personality, skills, and desires to 'find your passion.' In its own words, 'Are You Ready to Finally Find Your Passion? What's the secret to living a life full of passion, purpose and meaning? The secret is that there is no secret. The answer is hiding in plain sight. This book is different from other books of its kind, because it nudges you to look inside.In "Find Your Passion: 25 Questions You Must Ask Yourself" you'll dive into questions that will help you uncover what makes you come alive."

Rating: 2 Stars | **Category:** book

PROMOTED: THE PROVEN CAREER ACCELERATION FORMULA TO REACH THE TOP WITHOUT WORKING HARDER OR PLAYING OFFICE POLITICS -

http://www.amazon.com/Promoted-Acceleration-Formula-Without-Politics-ebook/dp/B01D92YLNM/

Author Bozi Dar gives you his career acceleration formula, so you can be the 10% that nabs the 70% (or is it 80%) of jobs out there. In its own words, 'Inside PROMOTED, Bozi shares the exact, step-by-step strategy that he used to achieve his amazing results, and that he teaches to top executives around the globe. As your trusted mentor, Bozi spotlights what you've been doing wrong, and he'll shatter some of your most cherished beliefs about your career. "

Rating: 2 Stars | **Category:** book

3
PERSONAL BRANDING

When author Tom Peters termed "The Brand Called You," he not only spawned an entire industry on personal branding, he presciently looked forward to the dawn of the Internet age. Today, to succeed in job search and career-building, you must have a personal website as well as engage with search and social media sites such as Google, Twitter, Facebook, LinkedIn, etc. But, behind it all, is your strategy of personal brand-building.

Here are the best free tools and resources on personal branding!

THE COMPLETE GUIDE TO BUILDING YOUR PERSONAL BRAND -

https://www.quicksprout.com/the-complete-guide-to-building-your-personal-brand/

> One of the very best online tutorials to the whole 'personal brand' thing. In its own words, 'This is an advanced guide to building your personal brand. There is a lot of information covering many different steps you can take to build your personal brand. However, not everything in this guide needs to be followed to reach your goals. Not everything in the guide applies to everyone so if you notice something that doesn't fit your vision or your goals it's okay. The purpose of this guide is to cover as much as possible about the process of building a personal brand. In the final chapter, we discuss why it's important to be yourself. You can take the information here as a guide, but use the information in your own way. Follow steps exactly or use certain information and create your own steps for finding success.'

Rating: 5 Stars | **Category:** tutorial

PERSONAL BRAND WORKBOOK (PDF) -

https://www.pwc.com/us/en/careers/campus/assets/img/programs/personal-brand-workbook.pdf

This is an interactive PDF / tutorial that helps you think through, define, and build out your personal brand image. Excellent. Prodcued by PWC (Price, Waterhouse, and Coopers & Lybrand). eBook format.

Rating: 5 Stars | **Category:** tutorial

TOM PETERS, 'THE BRAND CALLED YOU' - http://www.fastcompany.com/28905/brand-called-you

Written in 1997 at the dawn of the Internet Age, 'The Brand Called You' was prescient. Tom Peters saw the whole personal brand thing coming, and explained the basics. If you read one, and only one thing on personal branding, please read this.

Rating: 5 Stars | **Category:** article

BUILDING YOUR PERSONAL BRAND -
http://www.pwc.com/us/en/careers/campus/programs-events/personal-brand.html#overview

Focusing mainly on recent college graduates, this in-depth article overviews the stages of defining a personal brand. It helps you define who you are.

Rating: 4 Stars | **Category:** article

PERSONAL BRANDING BLOG - http://www.personalbrandingblog.com/

Yes, there's a portal online for everything, and yes, there's one for 'personal branding.' In its own words, 'The way we manage our careers is changing, due to the rise in competition and the introduction of web 2.0. In order to extend our reach, visibility and networking capabilities, we must turn to personal branding as our savior. In the digital age, our name is our only currency and by taking the first step reading this blog and consuming the information provided, you will have a competitive advantage in the marketplace. The content provided on this blog includes podcasts, interviews with experts, insightful articles, research reports, games and much more, for all your personal branding needs. Remember that YOU are the brand.'

Rating: 4 Stars | **Category:** resource

WIKIPEDIA ON PERSONAL BRANDING -
https://en.wikipedia.org/wiki/Personal_branding

Building on Tom Peter's 'Brand Called You,' Wikipedia is a great starting point for understanding personal branding. Then, put it into practice for defining your own image.

Rating: 3 Stars | **Category:** article

THE PERSONAL BRANDING BLOG - http://www.thepersonalbrandingblog.com/

Insights from William Aruda and the Reach-certified Personal branding strategists. In the words of Mr. Aruda, 'I launched this Blog with one objective - to provide unique insights and practical advice for using the power of personal branding to achieve your goals. It's dedicated to those who want to be wildly successful by maximizing what makes them unique, relevant and compelling.'

Rating: 3 Stars | **Category:** blog

PERSONAL BRANDING FOR DUMMIES - CHEAT SHEETS -
http://www.dummies.com/how-to/business-careers/Finding-a-Job/Personal-Branding/Personal-Branding-For-Dummies-Extras.html

Oops, take this 'sneak peak' into some of the worksheets and exercises in the 'Personal Branding for Dummies' book.

Rating: 3 Stars | **Category:** book

PERSONAL BRANDING AND MARKETING YOURSELF: THE THREE PS MARKETING TECHNIQUE AS A GUIDE TO CAREER EMPOWERMENT -
http://www.amazon.com/Personal-Branding-Marketing-Yourself-Empowerment/dp/0991505107/

Rita Balian Allen's 204 book focuses on the three PS's - preparing, packaging, and presenting. In her own words, ' Rita Balian Allen makes the case for personal branding as an essential ingredient for a successful career. For Rita and the many people who have sought her guidance, the Three Ps Marketing Technique has been the key. This technique PREPARES individuals to promote themselves by

PACKAGING their talents and accomplishments, showcasing them, and PRESENTING their value inside their organization as well as in their profession, industry or community. '

Rating: 3 Stars | **Category:** book

PERSONAL BRANDING FOR DUMMIES - http://www.amazon.com/Personal-Branding-Dummies-Susan-Chritton/dp/1118915550

It's a bit old, published in 2014, but Susan Chritton brings us one of the infamous 'dummies' books on building your personal brand. In its own words, 'This updated edition includes new information on expanding your brand through social media, online job boards, and communities, using the tried and true methods that are the foundation of personal branding. Marketing your skills and personality, and showing the rest of the world who you are, gives you a competitive edge. Whether you're looking for your first job, considering changing careers, or just want to be more viable and successful in your current career, this guide provides the step-by-step information you need to develop your personal brand.'

Rating: 3 Stars | **Category:** book

INTRODUCTION TO PERSONAL BRANDING: 10 STEPS TOWARD A NEW PROFESSIONAL YOU - http://www.amazon.com/Introduction-Personal-Branding-Toward-Professional-ebook/dp/B01A67OUIY

By author Mel Carson, 'In this Introduction to Personal Branding you will get a short crash course into what personal branding is, how to take your first steps toward perfecting your personal brand, and you will learn some actionable tactics you can employ immediately in order to start becoming more memorable within your career niche.'

Rating: 3 Stars | **Category:** book

YOU BRANDING: PERSONAL BRANDING BOOK - IT'S ALL ABOUT YOU - http://www.amazon.com/YOU-BRANDING-Personal-Branding-about-ebook/dp/B00HSRCQ64/

Mike Atack takes the 'You' and puts it into personal branding in this 2015 book. The book is a 'deep dive' into defining your personal brand.

Rating: 2 Stars | **Category:** book

4
RESUMES

There are sites where you can search for a job, a sort of "help wanted" on the Web. Ranging from Craig's List to CareerBuilder to Indeed and beyond, these sites allow you to look for job openings posted by employers. They also often have good tutorials and tips on the job search and career-building process. In addition, you can upload your own resume to these sites and be "findable" by headhunters and hiring managers.

Here are the best free tools and resources on resumes and job search!

ZIPRECRUITER - https://www.ziprecruiter.com/

> Artificial Intelligence, meet job search. Job search, meet AI. And then comes the singularity, Skynet, the terminator. But before all that happens: 'I'm Phil, a first-of-its-kind artificial intelligence designed to find you a job. I can search 6 million jobs in less than 1 second.
>
> Phil Try me.'
>
> **Rating:** 4 Stars | **Category:** service

INDEED.COM - http://www.indeed.com/

> Indeed was one of the first, if not the first, super job site. It consolidates job listings from other engines and attempts to bring them to you all in one place. Strongest in technology jobs. Don't miss their 'job search tools' which can alert you when new jobs are posted, etc.
>
> **Rating:** 4 Stars | **Category:** service

CREATE A RESUME ON MONSTER - http://resume.monster.com/

Post your resume on Monster today and make it searchable to employers. It's easy! You can upload your resume or start a new one by building a resume with Monster's Resume Builder. Also has information and tutorials on HOW to write a strong online resume.

Rating: 4 Stars | **Category:** service

THE LADDERS - https://www.theladders.com/

Another job search and resume-posting site. It has a great algorithm, bla, bla, bla. In their own words: 'Our services are designed to put professionals back in the driver seat, providing them with the right tools, insights and connections they need to thrive. Looking to change jobs? We'll leverage recruiter's search patterns to get you the 'Inside Lead' on exclusive job listings - often before they're even posted. Our powerful job-matching algorithm finds the most relevant job opportunities for you saving you time, and making your job-search efficient and effective.' Try it out.

Rating: 3 Stars | **Category:** service

RESUME.COM - https://www.resume.com/

Resume.com is a free resume hosting and job service. You can upload and edit your resume online, or use our easy wizard to create a new one. They also provide free resume hosting so employers instantly can view, download and print your resume no matter where they are or what platform they are using.

Rating: 3 Stars | **Category:** service

RESUME BUILDER - https://www.livecareer.com/

Resume builders are pretty much a dime a dozen. This site has that, plus some information on how to interview, career tests, how to build a cover letter, etc. So while, yes, it is a free resume builder site, it is also a question and answer site on the job hunt.

Rating: 3 Stars | **Category:** service

SUPER RESUME - http://www.super-resume.com/

Super-Resume.com grew from that frustration. They want to help you build the perfect resume effortlessly. Better than that, they also want to help you with your personal job hunt. The site's main function is RESUME TEMPLATES. Answer questions, and presto it creates a resume for you.

Rating: 3 Stars | **Category:** service

RESUME QUICKLY - http://www.resume-quickly.com/

Building a resume has never been so quick and easy, according to Resume Quickly. Their free resume builder is optimized to make the resume building process as fast as possible. Select a template, answer some questions, and PRESTO resume.

Rating: 3 Stars | **Category:** service

DICE.COM - http://www.dice.com/

Another job search site, focused on technology.

Rating: 3 Stars | **Category:** service

CAREER BUILDER - http://www.careerbuilder.com/

CareerBuilder is one of the largest online job site in the U.S., but it's more than just a job board. The mega site has infomration on resumes, cover letters, and pointers to more job-search resources. You can upload your resume to their database, plus peruse a detailed job-search process FAQ.

Rating: 3 Stars | **Category:** service

ERESUMES - http://www.eresumes.com/

eRsumes explains all you need to know about writing and distributing resumes and cover letters that will knock the socks off the recruiters, HR people and computers (yes, computers!) that read your resume. It's a little salesy, as they promote ResumeEdge - but ignore some of that, and you can learn a lot about resume-writing.

Rating: 2 Stars | **Category:** service

MONSTER.COM - http://www.monster.com/

Monster.com is dedicated to making make the job search process simple—and stress free. Their job search engine is built with powerful technology that aims to match the right job opportunities with the right people. To find the latest and most relevant job openings, simply browse by job title, company, city or state. Or become a member to get the first alerts on jobs you'll like.

Rating: Stars | **Category:** service

5
CONTENT MARKETING

Content is king, jack, and queen in terms of Internet marketing. For effective personal brand-building online, you'll need a lot of content. You'll need to share both your own content and content produced by others.

Here are the best free tools and resources on content marketing for career-building!

YOUTUBE TOOLS - http://bitly.com/ytcreatecorner

> YouTube has done more and more to make it easier to publish and promote videos. This page lists six tools: YouTube Capture, YouTube Editor, Captions, Audio Library, Slideshow and YouTube Analytics. All of them are fantastic, free tools about YouTube by YouTube.
>
> **Rating:** 5 Stars | **Category:** resource

BUZZSUMO - http://buzzsumo.com/

> Buzzsumo is a 'buzz' monitoring tool for social media. Input a website (domain) and/or a topic and see what people are sharing across Facebook, Twitter, Google+ and other social media. Great for link-building (because what people link to is what they share), and also for social media.
>
> **Rating:** 5 Stars | **Category:** tool

YOUTUBE CREATOR HUB - http://youtube.com/yt/creators

> Help center for those creating YouTube content. Learn how to better edit your videos, get them up on YouTube, etc. Has lessons on growing your audience, boot camp, and how to get viewers and even how to earn money via YouTube.

Rating: 5 Stars | **Category:** resource

FEEDLY - http://feedly.com/

Feedly is a newsreader integrated with Google+ or Facebook. It's useful for social media because you can follow important blogs or other content and share it with your followers. It can also spur great blog ideas.

Rating: 5 Stars | **Category:** resource

CREATIVE COMMONS SEARCH - http://search.creativecommons.org

Another resource to find royalty-free images, clip art, sound and music to share or utilize with other content. Great way to find shareable images to embed into blog posts.

Rating: 4 Stars | **Category:** resource

GOOGLE EMAIL ALERTS - https://www.google.com/alerts

Use Google to alert you by email for search results that matter to you. Input your company name, for example, to see when new web pages, blog posts, or other items surface on the web. Enter your target keywords to keep an eye on yourself and your competitors. Part of the Gmail system.

Rating: 4 Stars | **Category:** service

TAG BOARD - https://tagboard.com/

Hashtags have moved beyond Twitter. This amazing cool tool allows you to take a hashtag and browse Facebook and Twitter and Instagram, etc., so see posts that relate to that hashtag. Then you can find related tags. Oh, and you can use it as a content discovery tool, too.

Rating: 4 Stars | **Category:** tool

GOOGLE NEWS - https://news.google.com/

Excellent for reputation management as well as keeping up-to-date on specific keywords that matter to you and your business. First, sign in to your Google account or gmail. Second, customize Google news for your interest. Third, monitor your reputation as well as topics that matter to you. Go Google!

Rating: 4 Stars | **Category:** service

COMPFIGHT - http://compfight.com

Unclear where the name comes from, but no matter. This incredible tool allows you to search for royalty-based and royalty-free images. Great for finding images for blogging and posting to social media. Quickly locate royalty-free images!

Rating: 4 Stars | **Category:** service

YOUTUBE CAPTURE - https://youtube.com/capture

YouTube Capture is an app for your mobile phone, which makes it easy to capture and edit videos right on your phone. Imagine you are a marketer / retailer and you want to use your phone to easily capture customer interactions, and upload (quickly / easily) to YouTube. Get the picture?

Rating: 4 Stars | **Category:** tool

FOTER - http://foter.com

Add some color (or monochrome) to your blog posts with Foter. Search over 200 million high-quality, free, downloadable stock photos. Don't forget to copy and paste photo attribution credits included with the images details into your blog post.

Rating: 4 Stars | **Category:** resource

PHOTOPIN - http://photopin.com

Get in the habit of creating blog posts with images by using PhotoPin. PhotoPin searches millions of Creative Commons photos and allows you to preview, download any of multiple sizes to upload into your posts, and provides handy cut and paste HTML for attribution, a small price to pay for royalty-free images. Adding images to your blog posts doesn't get any easier than this.

Rating: 4 Stars | **Category:** service

WINDOWS MOVIE MAKER - http://bitly.com/windowsmov

For those on the Windows platform, Movie Maker is the goto free program to edit videos for YouTube and other platforms.

Rating: 3 Stars | **Category:** tool

DRUMUP - http://drumup.io/

DrumUp discovers and helps you share great content to your social media accounts

so you can start meaningful conversations with your followers. In simple words, it crawls the Web so you don't have to, and then you take that 'scraped' content and can share it to your followers. Efficiency, anyone?

Rating: 3 Stars | **Category:** tool

EASELY - http://easel.ly

Use thousands of templates and design objects to easily create infographics for your blog.

Rating: 3 Stars | **Category:** tool

MEME GENERATOR - http://memegenerator.net

Memes are shareable photos, usually with text. But how do you create them? Why, use memegenerator.net. Oh, and if you visit this site, you will spend about half an hour just laughing at stupid, funny memes. Now, get back to work, Keanu Reeves.

Rating: 3 Stars | **Category:** tool

ADDICTOMATIC - http://addictomatic.com

Nifty way to enter your company name or keyword and view a 'snapshot' of what's buzzing across multiple popular sources. Most useful for monitoring online reputation, admittedly at a high level of generality.

Rating: 3 Stars | **Category:** tool

RENOUN - http://renoun.io/

Similar to the defunct Topsy, this search engine finds NEW content especially articles on the Internet. You can search by keyword. It also shows you social shares.

Rating: 3 Stars | **Category:** service

SLIDESHARE - http://www.slideshare.net/

PowerPoint slides for the Web. Create a "deck," upload it to SlideShare and have a) a place to put content in slide format, and b) a platform that can also lead to discoverability. PowerPoint on the Web, PowerPoint gone social.

Rating: 3 Stars | **Category:** tool

WHAT DO YOU LOVE? - http://www.wdyl.com/

Despite its name, What do you love? is really an interesting monitoring service by Google. Type in a keyword that you want to 'monitor' and Google will build out all sorts of searches and monitoring tools. It's very cool, but we're not completely sure why it's called "What do you love?"

Rating: 3 Stars | **Category:** tool

MENTION - https://mention.com/en/

Similar to Google Alerts. Enter your email address and get free email alerts when topics are mentioned. For example, use your company name (personal name) and monitor your reputation online.

Rating: 3 Stars | **Category:** service

YOUTUBE EDITOR - https://www.youtube.com/editor

While there is Microsoft Windows Movie Maker and Apple iMovie, there is also a free YouTube editor for your videos. Not incredibly powerful, but free and easy to use 'in the cloud.'

Rating: 3 Stars | **Category:** tool

POWTOON - http://www.powtoon.com/

PowToon provides animated video production using the freemium pricing model. Play around with it to create animated videos to present anything you want about your business. Paid plans available, but you can do some cool stuff for free.

Rating: 2 Stars | **Category:** tool

INFO.GRAM - https://infogr.am

Another free way to create infographics and charts. Free plan is limited to 10 infographics, 10 uploaded images, no private sharing and no downloads or live connections.

Rating: 2 Stars | **Category:** tool

PIKTOCHART - http://piktochart.com

Free infographic creator. Useful for blogging and creating 'link bait' for link building.

Rating: 2 Stars | **Category:** tool

6

SEO BASICS

Search Engine Optimization (SEO) is the art and science of propelling your blog, your personal website, your infographic or other item to the top of Google or Bing. It is also highly relevant to understand which videos get to the top of YouTube, as well as which resumes get to the top of CareerBuilder or Monster searches, or which profiles get to the top of LinkedIn searches. It's a huge topic (hence I have a complete book on SEO called the *SEO Fitness Workbook* on Amazon), but here are the highlights.

Here are the best free tools and resources on SEO for job search and career-building!

GOOGLE SEO STARTER GUIDE - http://bit.ly/google-seo-starter

> This is the one, and only, really good resource by Google that is an official guide to what to do when, how, where and why for SEO. It covers mainly 'on page' SEO but definitely identifies basic tasks to accomplish on your website. Highly recommended.
>
> **Rating:** 5 Stars | **Category:** resource

UBERSUGGEST - http://ubersuggest.org

> Do you love Google suggest (the drop-down suggestions displayed when you type into Google)? It's great for keyword discovery. Ubersuggest is even better - it does a variety of things to provide all sorts of keyword suggestions. So it's a wonderful keyword discovery tool!
>
> **Rating:** 5 Stars | **Category:** tool

SEOCENTRO META TAG ANALYZER - http://seocentro.com/tools/search-engines/metatag-analyzer.html

SEOCentro designed this Meta Tag analysis tool to help webmasters analyze their web pages. This tool analyzes not only Meta Tags but where your keywords are positioned on the page, plus provides information on keyword density. When using Firefox, use CTRL+F to highlight your keywords in the results. In doing so, you can quickly check to see if a target keyword is well positioned vis-a-vis important tags like the TITLE or META DESCRIPTION tag.

Rating: 5 Stars | **Category:** tool

GOOGLE ADWORDS KEYWORD PLANNER - http://adwords.google.com/keywordplanner

Who got the data? Google got the data. Use the Keyword Planner for keyword discovery for both SEO and AdWords, but be sure to know how to use it. Not the easiest user interface, and remember it ONLY gives data for EXACT match types.

Rating: 5 Stars | **Category:** tool

SEARCH ENGINE LAND - http://searchengineland.com/

Search Engine Land is a news and information site covering search engine marketing, searching issues and the search engine industry and is led by journalist Danny Sullivan, one of the world's foremost search experts.

Rating: 5 Stars | **Category:** portal

GOOGLE SEARCH CONSOLE (WEBMASTER TOOLS) - https://www.google.com/webmasters/

Google Webmaster Tools provides detailed reports about your pages' visibility on Google. To get started, simply add and verify your site and begin seeing information right away. Get Google's view of your site and diagnose problems. See how Google crawls and indexes your site and learn about specific problems they're having accessing it. Discover your link and query traffic. Also contains an extensive education section with videos and articles to help you get found on Google.

Rating: 5 Stars | **Category:** tool

RELATED KEYWORDS - http://pagerank.net/related-keywords

Related Keywords enables you to identify related keywords and search terms that are closely related for your SEO optimization efforts. One of the FEW tools that's good for finding synonyms: lawyer vs. attorney, class vs. course, etc.

Rating: 5 Stars | **Category:** tool

GOOGLE WEBMASTER ACADEMY -
http://support.google.com/webmasters/answer/6001102

Google's learning site for SEO. Basic stuff, and a bit salesy, but a good starting point. Just remember who's talking - Google - and take it all with a grain of salt.

Rating: 5 Stars | **Category:** resource

OPENLINKPROFILER - http://openlinkprofiler.org

FREE tool for backlink analysis. Input your site, or that of a competitor, and see NEW links to that site. What's great is that it focuses on newly found links, not just all links, so that gives it a unique niche in the crowded field of backlink analysis tools. It also alerts to you to anchor texts and suspicious links.

Rating: 5 Stars | **Category:** tool

SEARCH ENGINE WATCH - http://searchenginewatch.com/

Search Engine Watch provides tips and information about searching the web, analysis of the search engine industry and help to site owners trying to improve their ability to be found in search engines. One of the leading websites for those in the SEO industry.

Rating: 5 Stars | **Category:** portal

GOOGLE GLOBAL MARKET FINDER - http://translate.google.com/globalmarketfinder

This is a new and different spin on the Google keywords tool. You can use it to browse keyword trends by countries, and you can drill down into synonyms based on the primary Google keyword tool. In some ways it's just a cooler, faster way to generate a list of keyword synonyms even if you aren't really interested in geography. Check it out, it's a COOL TOOL.

Rating: 5 Stars | **Category:** tool

SERPSTAT - http://sg.serpstat.com

Yet another amazing and fun tool based on Google suggest / suggested searches. Enter your keyword and brainstorm keyword ideas. Allows you to select Google top level domain (e.g., google.com, google.co.uk) for non-US search suggestions.

Rating: 5 Stars | **Category:** tool

GOOGLE KEYWORD PLANNER - https://adwords.google.com/KeywordPlanner

This is Google's keyword planner. It has now become the primary Google-based tool for keyword research. Be sure to watch Jason's YouTube video on how to use it, as the user interface leaves much to be desired! Still, it is the best tool for researching keyword volume vs. value (CPC) data.

Rating: 5 Stars | **Category:** tool

AHREFS - https://ahrefs.com/

AHrefs takes its name from the A HREF element/attribute (i.e., HTML hyperlink tag). This tool helps you investigate links and link-building issues for any website. A useful tool to use in companion with Open Site Explorer. You can also use it to reverse engineer competitor keywords.

Rating: 5 Stars | **Category:** tool

GOOGLE ANALYTICS - http://google.com/analytics

Google Analytics is an enterprise-class web analytics solution which provides detailed insights into your website traffic and marketing effectiveness. Powerful features let you see and analyze your traffic data to be more prepared to write better-targeted ads, strengthen marketing initiatives and create higher converting websites.

Rating: 5 Stars | **Category:** tool

BUZZSUMO - http://buzzsumo.com/

Buzzsumo is a 'buzz' monitoring tool for social media. Input a website (domain) and/or a topic and see what people are sharing across Facebook, Twitter, Google+ and other social media. Great for link-building (because what people link to is what they share), and also for social media.

Rating: 5 Stars | **Category:** tool

MOZ: OPEN SITE EXPLORER - https://moz.com/researchtools/ose/

This wonderful tool tells you who links to whom on the Internet. Enter a URL and the tool will then identify backlinks to that URL. Input your own website and check up how many links you have; enter a competitor, and 'reverse engineer' who links to them.

Rating: 5 Stars | **Category:** tool

TITLE TAG EVALUATION TOOL -
http://nightbirdwebsolutions.com/title_creator_tool.php

This tool will evaluate how your existing Title tag relates to the content on the page, and it can suggest an order for the words based upon your content. The tool can also evaluate a new web page title to compare to an existing title.

Rating: 4 Stars | **Category:** tool

SEO TAG COUNTER TOOLS - http://nightbirdwebsolutions.com/tools/title-description-tag-free-counter-tool

The TITLE tag should be less than 69 visible characters. The META DESCRIPTION should be less than 155 characters. This free tool allows you to input your text and count it automatically. Great for using as you write these two important META TAGS for SEO.

Rating: 4 Stars | **Category:** tool

SEARCH ENGINE LAND'S GUIDE TO SEO - http://searchengineland.com/guide/seo

Search Engine Land is clearly the top blog on search engine optimization. They provide this in-depth and pretty useful guide to SEO for their readership. They have a periodic table of SEO factors, which is a completely bizarre way to explain factors that have different ranks. But, oh well, they failed chemistry in High School but paid attention in math. This guide is a useful, basic guide to the subject.

Rating: 4 Stars | **Category:** tutorial

SOLO SEO LINK SEARCH TOOL - http://soloseo.com/tools/linkSearch.html

This simple, but nifty tool, will take a target keyword and generate a list of Google searches for blogs, catalogs, and other sorts of sites. Very simple, but very useful as a starting point on your link building exercise!

Rating: 4 Stars | **Category:** tool

SOOVLE - http://soovle.com

Let the web help - generate your keywords, that is. Type a keyword or phrase that interests you for SEO into Soovle and this nifty tool will generate phrase upon phrase of helper keywords. Very useful for idea generation and blogging.

Rating: 4 Stars | **Category:** tool

LINK BUILDING QUERY GENERATOR - http://tools.buzzstream.com/link-building-query-generator

Another input keywords and generate Google or Bing link tools. It creates an easy to use first step, but then you have to do the hard work to go and look for all those link targets!

Rating: 4 Stars | **Category:** tool

MAJESTIC SEO - https://majestic.com/

This company provides some pretty good link checking tools. Nothing that you really can't get from other sites, in easier-to-use format. But still if you are really researching who links to whom - yourself vs. competitors, this tool is free and worth a look.

Rating: 4 Stars | **Category:** tool

KEYWORD TOOL - https://serps.com/tools/keywords

Input your keyword or a keyword phrase, and this nifty - new - tool gives you many of the related phrases. Of note: it gives you volume and value information, which is better than many of these 'suggest' type of tools.

Rating: 4 Stars | **Category:** tool

SEOCENTRO KEYWORD DENSITY TOOL - http://seocentro.com/tools/seo/keyword-density.html

One element critical to SEO success is having good keyword density. A page that has good keyword density - such as three to seven percent of content - will outrank a page with lower density, all things considered. However, you also don't want to go overboard and have too many keywords. Input a web URL into this tool and it generates a cool 'keyword cloud' as well as helping you see the density.

Rating: 4 Stars | **Category:** tool

HOW GOOGLE SEARCH WORKS - http://www.google.com/insidesearch/howsearchworks/thestory/

Have you ever wondered how Google works? This somewhat cheeky guide is by Google about Google. It's a beginner's guide to how Google crawls the Web, and how it ranks the results on the Google search response page. Beginner level, but the basics of SEO are incredibly important!

Rating: 3 Stars | **Category:** overview

QUICKSPROUT SEO GUIDE - http://www.quicksprout.com/the-advanced-guide-to-seo/

Billed as an 'Advanced' guide, this is really more of a basic or beginner's look at SEO. Like the MOZ guide, it overemphasizes technical SEO and underemphasizes content marketing.

Rating: 3 Stars | **Category:** tutorial

MOZ SEO Beginners Guide - https://moz.com/beginners-guide-to-seo

MOZ is one of the top providers of (paid) SEO tools. It provides this basic introductory tutorial to SEO. Aimed at beginners, and (over)emphasizes technical SEO. But, hey, it's free.

Rating: 3 Stars | **Category:** tutorial

Google SEO Cheat Sheet - http://googlewebmastercentral.blogspot.com/2013/03/cheat-sheet-for-friends-and-family.html

This Google Webmaster Here is Google's one page SEO cheat sheet. This is a VERY basic guide to SEO, especially on page. Note: it's a PDF file but sometimes it doesn't show up like that when you download it. So you may have to "tell" your PC / MAC that it's a PDF file.

Rating: 2 Stars | **Category:** book

7

BLOGS

For nearly every person who wants to build an online personal brand image for job search or career-building, having a personal website or blog is a necessity. While a blog is more about timely posts on industry topics and a personal website might be more on stable topics such as one's resume or one's skills, the reality is that they are very, very similar. Whether you call it a personal blog or a personal website, you'll need resources, tools, and tips to be a better blogger and a better website builder.

Here are the best free tools and resources on blogs and personal websites for job search and career-building!

YOAST - https://yoast.com/

Yoast is the No. 1 recommended SEO plugin for WordPress. Highly recommended, as it adds needed functionality to WordPress such as splitting the TITLE tag from the Post TITLE, META description, and a nice 'focus' tool to analyze how well your post is optimized for on page SEO vs. a target keyword.

Rating: 4 Stars | **Category:** tool

LINKEDIN PULSE - https://www.linkedin.com/pulse/

Need ideas for your next blog post? Look no further than LinkedIn Pulse where top business influencers post their thoughts daily. Even better, you can post to LinkedIin Pulse and become a LinkedIn superstar as well. Even even better: post to both LinkedIn Pulse and your own blog.

Rating: 4 Stars | **Category:** resource

TWEAK YOUR BIZ TITLE GENERATOR - http://tweakyourbiz.com/tools/title-generator/index.php

> Good blog post TITLES are critical. You should include your keywords for SEO purposes, but add some pizazz, some sex appeal, some please-click-me oomph. This nifty tool gets your ideas flowing for good TITLES.
>
> **Rating:** 4 Stars | **Category:** tool

SIMPLE GUIDE TO BUSINESS BLOGGING - http://simplybusiness.co.uk/microsites/guide-business-blogging

> Interactive step-by-step guide to business blogging. Comprised of key questions and linked resources from around the web with more information. Thoughtful and well constructed.
>
> **Rating:** 4 Stars | **Category:** resource

CREATIVE COMMONS SEARCH - http://search.creativecommons.org

> Another resource to find royalty-free images, clip art, sound and music to share or utilize with other content. Great way to find shareable images to embed into blog posts.
>
> **Rating:** 4 Stars | **Category:** resource

PORTENT CONTENT IDEA GENERATOR - http://portent.com/tools/title-maker

> Very fun and mind-provocative tool for content ideas and better blog titles. Enter some keywords and the tool will generate some funny titles. So start with keywords and then generate your amazingly, funny and hypnotic blog titles. These then become the HEADLINES on Google by which you can attract more clicks!
>
> **Rating:** 4 Stars | **Category:** tool

PHOTOPIN - http://photopin.com

Get in the habit of creating blog posts with images by using PhotoPin. PhotoPin searches millions of Creative Commons photos and allows you to preview, download any of multiple sizes to upload into your posts, and provides handy cut and paste HTML for attribution, a small price to pay for royalty-free images. Adding images to your blog posts doesn't get any easier than this.

Rating: 4 Stars | **Category:** service

BLOG TOPIC GENERATOR - http://hubspot.com/blog-topic-generator

If you're hurting for blog topic ideas, try this fun tool from HubSpot. Enter three nouns, then watch the tool generate a weeks worth of blog topics. If none of the generated topics pique your interest, hit the back key and try, try again until one does.

Rating: 4 Stars | **Category:** tool

FOTER - http://foter.com

Add some color (or monochrome) to your blog posts with Foter. Search over 200 million high-quality, free, downloadable stock photos. Don't forget to copy and paste photo attribution credits included with the images details into your blog post.

Rating: 4 Stars | **Category:** resource

BLOG POST HEADLINE ANALYZER - http://coschedule.com/headline-analyzer

Want to write better blog headlines? Use the Blog Post Headline Analyzer to get a feel for how effective your blog post headlines are. This tool analyzes entered headlines across numerous criteria including keywords, sentiment, structure, grammar, and readability to produce a headline score in an attractive graphical format. Try it and see.

Rating: 4 Stars | **Category:** tool

COMPFIGHT - http://compfight.com

Unclear where the name comes from, but no matter. This incredible tool allows you to search for royalty-based and royalty-free images. Great for finding images for blogging and posting to social media. Quickly locate royalty-free images!

Rating: 4 Stars | **Category:** service

ULTIMATE HEADLINE FORMULAS

SAVE TIME ON SOCIAL MEDIA WITH BUFFER. SCHEDULE YOUR FIRST POST NOW!

ULTIMATE HEADLINE FORMULAS - https://blog.bufferapp.com/headline-formulas

If you've wondered how to create headlines for blog posts, articles, emails, etc., which will entice readers to click and read on, this article gathers a gaggle of formulas from some of the best sources for headline writing in one place. It also includes a free, downloadable PDF of the best headline formulas.

Rating: 3 Stars | **Category:** article

WORDPRESS SEO TUTORIAL - http://yoast.com/articles/wordpress-seo

This is a very good guide for WordPress SEO using the Yoast plugin. It covers only the technical issues, however, but when combined with our classes and an understanding of keyword research, website structure, and off-page SEO link building - this guide is very helpful for crossing the t's and dotting the i's of a strong SEO-friendly WordPress website.

Rating: 3 Stars | **Category:** resource

8

LINKEDIN

If there is one social media network that nearly everyone recognizes as critical for job search and career-building, it's *Snapchat*. Oh, oops, I meant **LinkedIn** (https://www.linkedin.com). Especially if you are looking to build a career in any type of professional service such as accounting, computer programming, marketing, etc., LinkedIn is an absolute must. *Snapchat, not so much.*

Here are the best free tools and resources on LinkedIn for job search and career-building!

LINKEDIN HELP CENTER - https://www.linkedin.com/help/linkedin

Learn about all the different features on LinkedIn. From a brief overview to detailed tips, you'll find them here. Learn about profiles. Find out how to get a new job. Use LinkedIn on your mobile phone. Learn how to build your network. Get answers to your questions with Answers.

Rating: 5 Stars | **Category:** overview

HOOTSUITE - https://hootsuite.com/

Manage all of your social media accounts, including multiple Twitter profiles through HootSuite. HootSuite makes it easy to manage multiple users over various social media accounts and allows you to track statistics. LOVE THIS TOOL!

Rating: 5 Stars | **Category:** vendor

BUFFER - https://buffer.com/

Schedule tweets and other social media activity in the future. Competitor to Hootsuite.

Rating: 4 Stars | **Category:** tool

LINKEDIN LEARNING WEBINARS -
http://help.linkedin.com/app/answers/detail/a_id/530

LinkedIn hosts live learning webinars on a variety of timely LinkedIn topics. Alternatively, users can view pre-recorded sessions. Topics are designed for a variety of audiences including, job seekers, corporate communications professionals, and journalists.

Rating: 4 Stars | **Category:** resource

LINKEDIN COMPANY PAGES FAQ - http://linkd.in/1BbOokZ

Interested in setting up a business page on LinkedIn? Here's the official FAQ on LinkedIn company pages.

Rating: 4 Stars | **Category:** resource

RAPPORTIVE - http://rapportive.com

Rapportive is a Gmail plugin that works with LinkedIn (and other social media sites). So when you're exchanging email with someone, you can see their LinkedIn profile details. It's sort of a bye-bye privacy app that helps you know how 'important' someone is with whom you are interacting.

Rating: 4 Stars | **Category:** tool

OFFICIAL LINKEDIN BLOG - http://blog.linkedin.com

The official LinkedIn Blog...lots of detailed information on what's happening when, where, and how on LinkedIn by LinkedIn staff.

Rating: 4 Stars | **Category:** blog

SMALL BUSINESS GUIDE TO LINKEDIN -
http://simplybusiness.co.uk/microsites/linkedin-guide

> Interactive step-by-step guide to using LinkedIn for small business. Comprised of key questions and linked resources from around the web with more information. Follow this step-by-step guide and make LinkedIn an effective part of your marketing strategy.
>
> **Rating:** 4 Stars | **Category:** resource

LINKEDIN YOUTUBE CHANNEL - https://www.youtube.com/user/LinkedIn

> LinkedIn has some novel advertising opportunities. This is their official YouTube channel. It's pretty salesy, but has some useful information especially on marketing and sales aspects of LinkedIn.
>
> **Rating:** 4 Stars | **Category:** video

LINKEDIN PULSE - https://www.linkedin.com/pulse/

> Need ideas for your next blog post? Look no further than LinkedIn Pulse where top business influencers post their thoughts daily. Even better, you can post to LinkedIin Pulse and become a LinkedIn superstar as well. Even even better: post to both LinkedIn Pulse and your own blog.
>
> **Rating:** 4 Stars | **Category:** resource

LINKEDIN MOBILE - https://mobile.linkedin.com/

> LinkedIn has just a few tools, but if you are a power LinkedIn user, these tools can help you search LinkedIn from your Google toolbar, import your contacts and perform other functions to help leverage your network for LinkedIn marketing. Primarily for your phone.
>
> **Rating:** 3 Stars | **Category:** tool

LINKEDIN ON TWITTER - https://twitter.com/LinkedIn

Yes, LinkedIn is on Twitter. So follow LinkedIn on Twitter for instant updates on LinkedIn about LinkedIn.

Rating: 3 Stars | **Category:** resource

EXPORT LINKEDIN CONNECTIONS - https://www.linkedin.com/addressBookExport

If you have built up a huge list of LinkedIn connections, use this tool to export them. Backup has never been cooler.

Rating: 3 Stars | **Category:** tool

LINKEDIN ON FACEBOOK - http://facebook.com/LinkedIn

Is LinkedIn on Facebook? Doesn't that sound crazy? Connect with LinkedIn on Facebook for the funner side of business networking at the official LinkedIn page on Facebook.

Rating: 3 Stars | **Category:** resource

LINKEDIN PLUGINS - http://developer.linkedin.com/plugins

Want to cross-promote your LinkedIn page from your website? Here's how. Use this page to find the nifty, official LinkedIn plugins. Share on LinkedIn, or follow us on LinkedIn. If you are in HR, you can even have an 'apply' via LinkedIn button. Cool!

Rating: 3 Stars | **Category:** tool

SLIDESHARE - http://www.slideshare.net/

PowerPoint slides for the Web. Create a "deck," upload it to SlideShare and have a) a place to put content in slide format, and b) a platform that can also lead to discoverability. PowerPoint on the Web, PowerPoint gone social.

Rating: 3 Stars | **Category:** tool

9
FACEBOOK

Facebook (https://www.facebook.com) is ubiquitous. Everyone is on Facebook, or nearly everyone. That said, Facebook is about friends, family, and fun, which makes using it for job search or career-building a bit counter-intuitive. It's all about tailoring how you use Facebook to either fit the "vibe" of friends, family, and fun, or using Facebook as a gigantic rolodex of friends and family who can help you in your career if you approach them in the right way.

Here are the best free tools and resources on Facebook for job search and career-building!

FACEBOOK LIKE BUTTON FOR WEB - https://developers.facebook.com/docs/plugins/like-button

> The Facebook Like button lets a user share your content with friends on Facebook. When the user clicks the Like button on your site, a story appears in the user's friends' News Feeds with a link back to your website.
>
> **Rating:** 5 Stars | **Category:** tool

FACEBOOK HELP CENTER - http://facebook.com/help

> The 'missing' help pages on Facebook. Useful for learning everything on the king of social media. Links on advertising, business accounts, connect, Facebook places and more.
>
> **Rating:** 5 Stars | **Category:** overview

HOOTSUITE - https://hootsuite.com/

Manage all of your social media accounts, including multiple Twitter profiles through HootSuite. HootSuite makes it easy to manage multiple users over various social media accounts and allows you to track statistics. LOVE THIS TOOL!

Rating: 5 Stars | **Category:** vendor

FACEBOOK SOCIAL PLUGINS (LIKE BOXES AND BUTTONS) - http://developers.facebook.com/docs/plugins

Make it easy for your Facebook fans and fans-to-be to 'like' your company and Facebook pages you create. The best Facebook resource for all plugins to integrate Facebook with your website, including the Like, Share & Send Button, Comments, Follow Button and others.

Rating: 5 Stars | **Category:** tool

FACEBOOK ADVERTISING - http://facebook.com/advertising

Facebook advertising opportunities. Run text ads on Facebook by selecting the demographics of who you want to reach. Pay-per-click model.

Rating: 4 Stars | **Category:** overview

KEYHOLE - http://keyhole.co

This tool provides real-time social conversation tracking for Twitter, Facebook, and Instagram. Use this tool to measure conversations around your business, identify prospective clients and influencers talking about your services, and find relevant content. Enables tracking of hashtags, keywords, and URLs.

Rating: 4 Stars | **Category:** tool

LIKEALYZER - http://likealyzer.com

LikeAlyzer analyzes the Facebook Page you enter and provides a very simple, easy to read report even the most statistically averse will understand. Best of all, LikeAlyzer provides an overall score and recommendations on where/how to improve. Recommendations are customized and analysis is based on the metrics the company has found to be important: presence, dialogue, action and information.

Rating: 4 Stars | **Category:** tool

BUFFER - https://buffer.com/

Schedule tweets and other social media activity in the future. Competitor to Hootsuite.

Rating: 4 Stars | **Category:** tool

SOCIALOOMPH - https://www.socialoomph.com/

SocialOomph is a powerful free (and paid) suite of tools to manage and schedule your Twitter and Facebook posts. Imagine going to the beach, forgetting about the office, yet having 67 different Tweets auto-posted...that's what SocialOomph is about. Use technology to appear busy and Facebooking / Tweeting all the time.

Rating: 4 Stars | **Category:** tool

FACEBOOK PAGES HELP CENTER - https://facebook.com/help/281592001947683

Here it is. The help center for Facebook 'pages', where businesses, organizations, and brands live. Use this handy dandy resource from Facebook to answer your most basic questions - such as how to set up a page for a business, how to administer your page (e.g., comments, kicking users off and all that fun stuff), as well as how to manage admins. It is the first 'goto' page for help with Facebook Pages for business.

Rating: 4 Stars | **Category:** resource

IFTTT - https://ifttt.com

This app, If Then Then That, is a great tool for linking multiple social media accounts. It allows you to create 'recipes' that link your tools exactly the way you like them! For example: make a recipe that adds to a Google Apps spreadsheet every time a particular user uploads to Instagram - a great way to keep up with your competitors SMM strategies! With over 120 supported applications, the 'recipes' are endless, making this a good tool for your SMM strategies.

Rating: 4 Stars | **Category:** tool

TAG BOARD - https://tagboard.com/

Hashtags have moved beyond Twitter. This amazing cool tool allows you to take a hashtag and browse Facebook and Twitter and Instagram, etc., so see posts that relate to that hashtag. Then you can find related tags. Oh, and you can use it as a content discovery tool, too.

Rating: 4 Stars | **Category:** tool

FACEBOOK PAGE BASICS (FOR BUSINESS) - https://www.facebook.com/business/learn/facebook-page-basics

Confused by Facebook for Business? Have no fear, Learn How, Facebook's online learning center for businesses, is here. This easy-to-use resource, complete with videos, images and step-by-step instructions, answers businesses' frequently asked questions, like how to create a Page, and how to create a Custom Audience. Learn How content is organized to be flexible: use it in-depth, or as a reference library as questions arise.

Rating: 4 Stars | **Category:** tutorial

FACEBOOK FOR BUSINESS: MARKETING SOLUTIONS - https://www.facebook.com/marketing

Official pages on Facebook-approved 'best practices' for marketing your company on Facebook.

Rating: 4 Stars | **Category:** overview

SMALL BUSINESS GUIDE TO FACEBOOK - http://simplybusiness.co.uk/microsites/facebook-for-small-businesses

Interactive step-by-step flowchart to using Facebook for small business. Comprised of key questions and linked resources with more information. Chart is divided into different areas including goals and measurement, engagement, page management, Facebook ads, and advanced tips. Worth a look.

Rating: 4 Stars | **Category:** resource

DRUMUP - http://drumup.io/

DrumUp discovers and helps you share great content to your social media accounts

so you can start meaningful conversations with your followers. In simple words, it crawls the Web so you don't have to, and then you take that 'scraped' content and can share it to your followers. Efficiency, anyone?

Rating: 3 Stars | **Category:** tool

10
TWITTER

Do you use Twitter (https://twitter.com) for your career, should you, or could you? It depends. Twitter is a very, very noisy social media platform, yet it has unique features such as the ability to tweet to anyone, that make it powerful for job search and career-building. Plus, in many fields such as marketing, it's an absolute *must for trust*. In other industries, you can use Twitter not only as a *trust indicator* but as a way to chime in on industry topics and industry trade shows. Twitter is not just for Ryan Seacrest (@RyanSeacrest, 14.2 million followers)!

Here are the best free tools and resources on Twitter for job search and career-building!

HOOTSUITE - https://hootsuite.com/

> Manage all of your social media accounts, including multiple Twitter profiles through HootSuite. HootSuite makes it easy to manage multiple users over various social media accounts and allows you to track statistics. LOVE THIS TOOL!
>
> **Rating:** 5 Stars | **Category:** vendor

TWITTER ADVANCED SEARCH - https://twitter.com/search-advanced

> Search to see what others are saying about topics relevant and your organization's interests, before, during, after you use Twitter. Here's a nifty trick: Use the 'Near this place' field to find people in a city near you tweeting on a topic like 'pizza.' Great for local brands.
>
> **Rating:** 5 Stars | **Category:** tool

HASHTAGIFY.ME - http://hashtagify.me

Hashtagify.me allows you to search tens of millions of Twitter hashtags and quickly find the best ones for your needs based on popularity, relationships, languages, influencers and other metrics. Also useful for SEO link building and keyword discovery.

Rating: 5 Stars | **Category:** tool

BUZZSUMO - http://buzzsumo.com/

Buzzsumo is a 'buzz' monitoring tool for social media. Input a website (domain) and/or a topic and see what people are sharing across Facebook, Twitter, Google+ and other social media. Great for link-building (because what people link to is what they share), and also for social media.

Rating: 5 Stars | **Category:** tool

HASHTAGS.ORG - http://hashtags.org

Tool which attempts to organize the world's hashtags. Provides hashtag analytics for your brand, business, product, service, event or blog. Input words that matter to you, and Hashtags looks to see the trends on Twitter.

Rating: 4 Stars | **Category:** engine

KEYHOLE - http://keyhole.co

This tool provides real-time social conversation tracking for Twitter, Facebook, and Instagram. Use this tool to measure conversations around your business, identify prospective clients and influencers talking about your services, and find relevant content. Enables tracking of hashtags, keywords, and URLs.

Rating: 4 Stars | **Category:** tool

SMALL BUSINESS GUIDE TO TWITTER - http://simplybusiness.co.uk/microsites/twitter-for-small-businesses

Interactive step-by-step flowchart to using Twitter for small business. Comprised of key questions and linked resources with more information. Covers everything from very basic to advanced topics.

Rating: 4 Stars | **Category:** resource

TWITAHOLIC - http://twitaholic.com

Tracks the most popular Twitter users based on followers. Use this to find top tweeters - sort of a top 100, 200, 300, etc list for the Twitterdom. Also just a great way to find out who's really famous on Twitter. Katy Perry, anyone?

Rating: 4 Stars | **Category:** service

TWITONOMY - http://twitonomy.com

Twitonomy is a free online Twitter analytics tool which provides a wealth of information about all aspects of Twitter, including in-depth stats on any Twitter user, insights on your followers, mentions, favorites & retweets, and analytics on hashtags. It also lets you monitor tweets, manage your lists, download tweets & reports, and much more. Definitely worth checking out if Twitter is part of your social media strategy.

Rating: 4 Stars | **Category:** tool

TWITTER ANALYTICS - https://analytics.twitter.com

The official page for Twitter analytics and metrics. Sign up via Twitter, and learn how your tweets are doing!

Rating: 4 Stars | **Category:** tool

BUFFER - https://buffer.com/

Schedule tweets and other social media activity in the future. Competitor to Hootsuite.

Rating: 4 Stars | **Category:** tool

SOCIALOOMPH - https://www.socialoomph.com/

SocialOomph is a powerful free (and paid) suite of tools to manage and schedule your Twitter and Facebook posts. Imagine going to the beach, forgetting about the office, yet having 67 different Tweets auto-posted...that's what SocialOomph is about. Use technology to appear busy and Facebooking / Tweeting all the time.

Rating: 4 Stars | **Category:** tool

IFTTT - https://ifttt.com

This app, If Then Then That, is a great tool for linking multiple social media accounts. It allows you to create 'recipes' that link your tools exactly the way you like them! For example: make a recipe that adds to a Google Apps spreadsheet every time a particular user uploads to Instagram - a great way to keep up with your competitors SMM strategies! With over 120 supported applications, the 'recipes' are endless, making this a good tool for your SMM strategies.

Rating: 4 Stars | **Category:** tool

FOLLOWERWONK - https://moz.com/followerwonk/

Followerwonk helps you explore and grow your social graph. Dig deeper into Twitter analytics: Who are your followers? Where are they located? When do they tweet? Find and connect with new influencers in your niche. Use actionable visualizations to compare your social graph to others. Easily share your reports with the world. Brought to you by Moz.

Rating: 4 Stars | **Category:** tool

TWITTER HELP CENTER - https://support.twitter.com

Did you know Twitter has technical support? Yep, they do. It's relatively hidden, but here it is. It's more for users of Twitter, but it does have some juicy help for actual businesses on Twitter as well. Tweet, tweet, tweet.

Rating: 4 Stars | **Category:** resource

TAG BOARD - https://tagboard.com/

Hashtags have moved beyond Twitter. This amazing cool tool allows you to take a hashtag and browse Facebook and Twitter and Instagram, etc., so see posts that relate to that hashtag. Then you can find related tags. Oh, and you can use it as a content discovery tool, too.

Rating: 4 Stars | **Category:** tool

TAGDEF - https://tagdef.com

Looking to understand what a particular hashtag means? Use this nifty tool to define a hashtag and to research hashtags BEFORE you create or use them.

Rating: 4 Stars | **Category:** tool

TWEETDECK - https://tweetdeck.twitter.com

TweetDeck is your personal browser for staying in touch with what's happening now, connecting you with your contacts across Twitter, Facebook, MySpace, LinkedIn and more. Developed independently, now owned by Twitter.

Rating: 4 Stars | **Category:** service

BITLY - https://bitly.com

Bitly is a URL shortening service that will track your click-throughs. Very useful for email marketing, blogging, and Twitter.

Rating: 4 Stars | **Category:** service

11

OTHER NETWORKS

Search and *social media* for personal branding – both job search and career-building – are more than just Google (there's Bing! there's Yahoo!) and Facebook, Twitter, and LinkedIn (there's Instagram! there's Google+!). Here, with respect to Instagram, YouTube, Pinterest, Amazon, Snapchat, Google+, and Tumblr, is a cornucopia of job resources and tools (in alphabetical order).

Here are the best free tools and resources on other networks for job search and career-building!

AMAZON

CREATESPACE BY AMAZON - https://www.createspace.com/

CreateSpace, owned by Amazon, allows you to self-publish a book to both paperback and Kindle formats.

Rating: 5 Stars | **Category:** service

KDP ON AMAZON (KINDLE DIRECT PUBLISHING) - https://kdp.amazon.com/

One of the very best 'validations' that you are a 'helpful expert' is to publish a book. Amazon's Kindle platform makes this easier than ever. You can easily self-publish a book on Amazon. Here's where you get started.

Rating: 5 Stars | **Category:** service

GOOGLE+

GOOGLE MY BUSINESS (GOOGLE+ LOCAL / GOOGLE PLACES) HELP CENTER -
https://support.google.com/business#topic=4539639

A wonderful and rather hidden microsite in the Googleplex with many help topics to learn about, modify, and update your Google+ Local listings. Google Local begot Google Places begot Google+ Local begot Google My Business. You and I both wish Google would settle on a name for its local service!

Rating: 5 Stars | **Category:** resource

SMALL BUSINESS GUIDE TO GOOGLE+ -
http://simplybusiness.co.uk/microsites/googleplus-for-small-businesses

Interactive step-by-step flowchart to using Google+ for small business. Comprised of key questions and linked resources with more information. Chart is divided into different areas including set up, integration, and engagement. Worth a look.

Rating: 4 Stars | **Category:** resource

INSTAGRAM

TAG BOARD - https://tagboard.com/

Hashtags have moved beyond Twitter. This amazing cool tool allows you to take a hashtag and browse Facebook and Twitter and Instagram, etc., so see posts that relate to that hashtag. Then you can find related tags. Oh, and you can use it as a content discovery tool, too.

Rating: 4 Stars | **Category:** tool

IFTTT - https://ifttt.com

This app, If Then Then That, is a great tool for linking multiple social media accounts. It allows you to create 'recipes' that link your tools exactly the way you like them! For example: make a recipe that adds to a Google Apps spreadsheet every time a particular user uploads to Instagram - a great way to keep up with your competitors SMM strategies! With over 120 supported applications, the 'recipes' are endless, making this a good tool for your SMM strategies.

Rating: 4 Stars | **Category:** tool

INSTAGRAM FOR BUSINESS - https://business.instagram.com

Hey you're a business! Here's how to get on Instagram as a business, and use it to your advantage.

Rating: 4 Stars | **Category:** resource

INSTAGRAM MARKETING GUIDE - http://socialmediaexaminer.com/instagram-marketing-guide

This guide from Social Media Examiner isn't (just) for Instagram newbies, as it includes links to SME articles on topics like integrating video and running contests. There's something for just about everyone here, from the marketing strategist to the social media practitioner. Check it and see.

Rating: 4 Stars | **Category:** resource

SNAPWIDGET - http://snapwidget.com

Use this widget to quickly and easily embed an Instagram photos on your website or blog.

Rating: 4 Stars | **Category:** tool

LATERGRAMME - https://www.latergram.me/

Hootsuite for Instagram: schedule posts into the future. In this way, you can make your Instagram account "look" like it's always active, but you can manage it on a scheduled basis. Go to the beach or go shopping.

Rating: 3 Stars | **Category:** service

POSTRIS - http://postris.com/

An advanced, web-based Instagram dashboard for tracking and organizing your Instagram account and daily updates from leading publications and social networks. Helps users keep up with what is trending on Instagram

Rating: 3 Stars | **Category:** tool

PINTEREST

PINTEREST HELP TOPICS - https://help.pinterest.com/en/articles

Browse topic by topic through the Pinterest help pages. For example, learn the basics of what pins are and how to use them. Great for beginners.

Rating: 3 Stars | **Category:** resource

PINTEREST HELP CENTER - https://help.pinterest.com/en

Need help? Well, guess what, Pinterest has a robust help section, mainly for users but useful for you as a business marketer. You gotta know how they use it, to use it to market to them!

Rating: 3 Stars | **Category:** resource

PIN SEARCH - https://chrome.google.com/webstore/detail/pin-search-image-search-o/okiaciimfpgbpdhnfdllhdkicpmdoakm

An extension for Chrome browser that allows users to easily find related photos and information for photos posted on Pinterest.

Rating: 2 Stars | **Category:** service

CANVA - https://canva.com

This free image editing tool is optimized for Pinterest so all of your pins and boards look sleek. Also has an iPad app.

Rating: 3 Stars | **Category:** tool

PINTEREST BUSINESS GUIDES - https://business.pinterest.com/en/pinterest-guides

Downloadable business-friendly guides from Pinterest about how to use Pinterest effectively for your business.

Rating: 3 Stars | **Category:** resource

PINTEREST GOODIES - https://about.pinterest.com/en/browser-button

Made more for the end user than the business user, this is a resource by Pinterest about Pinterest. For example, both the iOS and Android apps are available here. Don't miss the 'Pin It' button which makes it easy to pin content from your browser, as well as widgets for your website to encourage Pinterest.

Rating: 4 Stars | **Category:** tool

PINGROUPIE - http://pingroupie.com

Use this tool to find group boards on Pinterest where you can join and contribute. Additionally, PinGroupie has options for sorting boards by popularity so you can quickly see those with the biggest following, or most pins or likes.

Rating: 3 Stars | **Category:** tool

PINTEREST RICH PINS - https://business.pinterest.com/rich-pins

Rich Pins are pins that include extra information on the pin itself. The six types of rich pins are: app, movie, recipe, article, product, and place. Use these six rich pins in addition to your 'pin it' link to further enhance your post for your viewers.

Rating: 4 Stars | **Category:** tool

PINTEREST TOOLS FOR BUSINESS - https://business.pinterest.com/en/tools

Yes, you wanted it. Yes, they created it: a one-stop resource of tools to help your business succeed on Pinterest. Has not only official Pinterest tools, but also a compilation of third party business-friendly tools to help you pin it, to win it.

Rating: 4 Stars | **Category:** tool

PINTEREST FOR BUSINESS - https://business.pinterest.com

Looking to 'get started' on Pinterest? Here is the official site on how a business page for Pinterest works.

Rating: 3 Stars | **Category:** resource

ULTIMATE PINTEREST MARKETING GUIDE - https://blog.kissmetrics.com/ultimate-pinterest-marketing-guide/

KISSmetrics has produced a landmark guide to how to use Pinterest for business. It's a great, basic read for the beginner.

Rating: 3 Stars | **Category:** article

PINTEREST FOR BUSINESS - http://www.businessnewsdaily.com/7552-pinterest-business-guide.html

Pinterest can be used to promote your business, especially if you reach one of the two intertwined demographics: young women and shoppers. This brief but meaty article explains how.

Rating: 3 Stars | **Category:** archive

PINTEREST ANALYTICS - https://business.pinterest.com/en/pinterest-analytics

Use this tool to easily see what people like from your Pinterest profile and what they pin from your website. Learn about your audience by viewing metrics and common interests. Great tool to analyze your Pinterest marketing strategy.

Rating: 4 Stars | **Category:** tool

PINTEREST PIN IT BUTTON - https://business.pinterest.com/en/pin-it-button

Want your business to be discovered on Pinterest? The Pin It button allows your customers to save what they like to Pinterest and shows their followers what they're interested in. An easy way to get referral traffic and what Pinterest calls, 'a button that works for you'.

Rating: 4 Stars | **Category:** tool

IFTTT - https://ifttt.com

This app, If Then Then That, is a great tool for linking multiple social media accounts. It allows you to create 'recipes' that link your tools exactly the way you like them! For example: make a recipe that adds to a Google Apps spreadsheet every time a particular user uploads to Instagram - a great way to keep up with your competitors SMM strategies! With over 120 supported applications, the 'recipes' are endless, making this a good tool for your SMM strategies.

Rating: 4 Stars | **Category:** tool

SNAPCHAT

SNAPCHAT - https://www.snapchat.com/

Snapchat is the new new thing, especially among the teenage set. It may or may not help you with your personal brand image online.

Rating: 5 Stars | **Category:** service

SNAPCHAT HELP CENTER - https://support.snapchat.com/en-US/

Yes, it exists! Despite what the teen set would have you to know, you can learn how to use Snapchat. Here are the 'secret' help files.

Rating: 4 Stars | **Category:** service

Tumblr

Tumblr - https://www.tumblr.com/

Look up in the sky! It's a blog, it's a social network, it's a subsidiary of Yahoo! Tumblr is all of the above, and especially if you're 'artsy,' it can be an excellent place for your blog content to live.

Rating: 5 Stars | **Category:** service

Tumblr Help - https://www.tumblr.com/help

Here are the help files on how to use Tumblr. Did you know you can have a primary and a secondary blog?

Rating: 4 Stars | **Category:** service

Tumblr Tutorials - http://unwrapping.tumblr.com/

Yes, of course, there's a Tumblr blog that collects tutorials on how to use Tumblr.

Rating: 4 Stars | **Category:** tutorial

YouTube

YouTube Tools - http://bitly.com/ytcreatecorner

YouTube has done more and more to make it easier to publish and promote videos. This page lists six tools: YouTube Capture, YouTube Editor, Captions, Audio Library, Slideshow and YouTube Analytics. All of them are fantastic, free tools about YouTube by YouTube.

Rating: 5 Stars | **Category:** resource

YOUTUBE CREATOR HUB - http://youtube.com/yt/creators

Help center for those creating YouTube content. Learn how to better edit your videos, get them up on YouTube, etc. Has lessons on growing your audience, boot camp, and how to get viewers and even how to earn money via YouTube.

Rating: 5 Stars | **Category:** resource

IMOVIE FOR MAC - https://apple.com/mac/imovie

Apple's free, downloadable movie / video editor. Great for making YouTube videos!

Rating: 4 Stars | **Category:** tool

YOUTUBE CAPTURE - https://youtube.com/capture

YouTube Capture is an app for your mobile phone, which makes it easy to capture and edit videos right on your phone. Imagine you are a marketer / retailer and you want to use your phone to easily capture customer interactions, and upload (quickly / easily) to YouTube. Get the picture?

Rating: 4 Stars | **Category:** tool

YOUTUBE ADVERTISING RESOURCES - https://www.youtube.com/yt/advertise/

YouTube wants you to advertise! But, it also hides some good free SEO-oriented resources here for how to use YouTube effectively. Worth a look, and a bookmark.

Rating: 4 Stars | **Category:** resource

YOUTUBE SPOTLIGHT - https://www.youtube.com/user/YouTube

Trying to understand YouTube? This is the official YouTube Channel by YouTube on YouTube. Use to to discover what's new and trending around the world from music to culture to Internet phenomena, must-watch videos from across YouTube, all in one place.

Rating: 4 Stars | **Category:** video

POPULAR ON YOUTUBE -

https://www.youtube.com/channel/UCF0pVplsI8R5kcAqgtoRqoA

An auto-generated collection of what's popular on YouTube, and - shall we say - 'going viral.' As a marketer, seek to observe and understand why things go viral and how to leverage the video popularity wave.

Rating: 4 Stars | **Category:** service

SMALL BUSINESS GUIDE TO YOUTUBE -

http://simplybusiness.co.uk/microsites/youtube-for-small-business

Interactive step-by-step flowchart to YouTube marketing. Comprised of key questions and linked resources with more information. Excellent resource. Worth a look.

Rating: 4 Stars | **Category:** resource

YOUTUBE HELP CENTER - http://support.google.com/youtube

The official help site for YouTube, conveniently located on Google. Google owns YouTube, but you already knew that.

Rating: 4 Stars | **Category:** overview

WINDOWS MOVIE MAKER - http://bitly.com/windowsmov

For those on the Windows platform, Movie Maker is the goto free program to edit videos for YouTube and other platforms.

Rating: 3 Stars | **Category:** tool

YOUTUBE CREATOR ACADEMY - http://creatoracademy.withgoogle.com

Learn tips and tricks from the YouTube pros to maximize your corporate YouTube page. Expert videos, tests, and even a way to 'meet' other YouTube content creators. Fun, friendly, and free.

Rating: 3 Stars | **Category:** resource

TUBECHOP - http://tubechop.com

Enter a YouTube video URL, watch it, and 'chop it' at the moment you want a user to see. This way, you can share just the portion of a video you want, rather than forcing people to watch a long boring intro or other non-relevant content.

Rating: 3 Stars | **Category:** tool

WIDEO - http://wideo.co

An online video maker, similar to iMovie or Windows Movie Maker.

Rating: 3 Stars | **Category:** tool

YOUTUBE EMBED TOOL (CUSTOMIZED) - http://www.classynemesis.com/projects/ytembed/

Sure you can embed YouTube videos directly, but this cool tool allows you to optimize and customize what you want to do. For example, start at a particular moment, or add easy social share buttons.

Rating: 3 Stars | **Category:** tool

YOUTUBE CREATOR STUDIO ANDROID APP - http://bit.ly/1dqVLc2

Use YouTube Creator Studio to manage your channel from your Android phone. Great when you're on the go. For iTunes version go to http://bit.ly/yc-iphone.

Rating: 3 Stars | **Category:** tool

YOUTUBE BLOG - http://youtube-global.blogspot.com

The official YouTube blog. If YouTube is important to you - whether as a video hosting service and/or as a social media method to connect with customers - here is where you find the inside scoop on Google's YouTube service.

Rating: 3 Stars | **Category:** blog

YouTube Help Channel - https://youtube.com/youtubehelp

More for general users than for marketers, the YouTube Help channel has informative videos on how to 'use' YouTube. That said, if you know how your customers use YouTube, you can become a better marketer towards them. Includes tutorials, troubleshooting, and tips. Never stop learning!

Rating: 3 Stars | **Category:** resource

YouTube Help Forum - https://productforums.google.com/forum/#!forum/youtube

The new and improved forum by and about YouTube - user-generated content, helpful tips and pointers from official YouTubers. This is your 'goto' site if you want to post a question for the community and hopefully get some help.

Rating: 3 Stars | **Category:** resource

YouTube on Facebook - https://www.facebook.com/youtube

Facebook is on YouTube, and so YouTube is on Facebook. Just 'Like" YouTube on Facebook and stay up-to-date with happenings on YouTube (on Faceboook). It's recursive!

Rating: 3 Stars | **Category:** resource

YouTube Editor - https://www.youtube.com/editor

While there is Microsoft Windows Movie Maker and Apple iMovie, there is also a free YouTube editor for your videos. Not incredibly powerful, but free and easy to use 'in the cloud.'

Rating: 3 Stars | **Category:** tool

YouTube Advertisers Channel - https://youtube.com/user/advertise

Interested in advertising on YouTube? This is the official channel with tons of useful, if salesy, content on why and how to advertise your products or services on YouTube. If you're into advertising, check out the 'Ads Leaderboard,' which highlights top ads month by month.

Rating: 3 Stars | **Category:** video

YOUTUBE CREATORS BLOG - http://youtubecreator.blogspot.com

The official YouTube blog by and about YouTube partners. You can pick up some good tips on YouTube marketing here, plus learn some ins and outs from YouTube superstars. Plus it's just plain fun to see what the YouTube famous are up to.

Rating: 3 Stars | **Category:** blog

REELSEO VIDEO MARKETER'S GUIDE - http://www.reelseo.com/

A leading resource for news, analysis, tips and trends for the online video and Internet marketing industries. Their videologists and columnists offer expert advice, guidance, and commentary about the world of online video to guide Internet marketers and video content producers on best practices and online video services that suit their needs.

Rating: 2 Stars | **Category:** portal

POWTOON - http://www.powtoon.com/

PowToon provides animated video production using the freemium pricing model. Play around with it to create animated videos to present anything you want about your business. Paid plans available, but you can do some cool stuff for free.

Rating: 2 Stars | **Category:** tool

YOUTUBE (BRAND) CHANNELS - https://support.google.com/youtube/topic/4601639

Brand channels on YouTube have an advertising component, but many of the items on this page are applicable to regular channels on YouTube as well. So this is a useful 'how to' article on managing a brand page on YouTube.

Rating: 2 Stars | **Category:** article

YOUTUBE ON TWITTER - https://twitter.com/youtube

YouTube's official Twitter profile (@YouTube). So does Twitter have an official channel on YouTube? This could get weird.

Rating: 2 Stars | **Category:** resource

YOUTUBE ON GOOGLE+ - https://plus.google.com/+youtube

If you are really into YouTube, follow them on social media. Here is their Google+ page.

Rating: 1 Stars | **Category:** resource

12
MONITORING

In life sometimes all you have is your "good word," and on the Internet sometimes all you have is your "reputation." You need to monitor your personal brand image reputation, as well as measure your performance.

Here are the best free tools and resources on reputation management for job search and career-building!

SOCIAL MENTION - http://socialmention.com

> Social Mention is a social media search and analysis platform that aggregates user generated content from across the universe into a single stream of information. Use it to search Twitter, Facebook, and other social media sites for mentions in addition to other useful information like keywords used to search for topics entered.
>
> **Rating:** 5 Stars | **Category:** engine

FEEDLY - http://feedly.com/

> Feedly is a newsreader integrated with Google+ or Facebook. It's useful for social media because you can follow important blogs or other content and share it with your followers. It can also spur great blog ideas.
>
> **Rating:** 5 Stars | **Category:** resource

BUZZSUMO - http://buzzsumo.com/

> Buzzsumo is a 'buzz' monitoring tool for social media. Input a website (domain) and/or a topic and see what people are sharing across Facebook, Twitter,

Google+ and other social media. Great for link-building (because what people link to is what they share), and also for social media.

Rating: 5 Stars | **Category:** tool

GOOGLE EMAIL ALERTS - https://www.google.com/alerts

Use Google to alert you by email for search results that matter to you. Input your company name, for example, to see when new web pages, blog posts, or other items surface on the web. Enter your target keywords to keep an eye on yourself and your competitors. Part of the Gmail system.

Rating: 4 Stars | **Category:** service

GOOGLE NEWS - https://news.google.com/

Excellent for reputation management as well as keeping up-to-date on specific keywords that matter to you and your business. First, sign in to your Google account or gmail. Second, customize Google news for your interest. Third, monitor your reputation as well as topics that matter to you. Go Google!

Rating: 4 Stars | **Category:** service

KEYHOLE - http://keyhole.co

This tool provides real-time social conversation tracking for Twitter, Facebook, and Instagram. Use this tool to measure conversations around your business, identify prospective clients and influencers talking about your services, and find relevant content. Enables tracking of hashtags, keywords, and URLs.

Rating: 4 Stars | **Category:** tool

MENTION - https://mention.com/en/

Similar to Google Alerts. Enter your email address and get free email alerts when topics are mentioned. For example, use your company name (personal name) and monitor your reputation online.

Rating: 3 Stars | **Category:** service

WHAT DO YOU LOVE? - http://www.wdyl.com/

Despite its name, What do you love? is really an interesting monitoring service by Google. Type in a keyword that you want to 'monitor' and Google will build out all sorts of searches and monitoring tools. It's very cool, but we're not completely sure why it's called "What do you love?"

Rating: 3 Stars | **Category:** tool

ADDICTOMATIC - http://addictomatic.com

Nifty way to enter your company name or keyword and view a 'snapshot' of what's buzzing across multiple popular sources. Most useful for monitoring online reputation, admittedly at a high level of generality.

Rating: 3 Stars | **Category:** tool

www.ingramcontent.com/pod-product-compliance
Lightning Source LLC
Chambersburg PA
CBHW080725190526
45169CB00006B/2515